I0055412

INDIE AUTHOR MAGAZINE

HELLO AND WELCOME!

I'm Indie Annie, and I'm thrilled you're reading this gorgeous full-color version of IAM. Did you know that you can also access all the information, education, and inspiration in our app? It's available on both the iOS App Store and Google Play. And for those that prefer to listen to me read articles, you can pop over to Spotify or our website. Happy Reading!

X

IndieAuthorMagazine.com

Download on the **App Store**

GET IT ON **Google Play**

Spotify

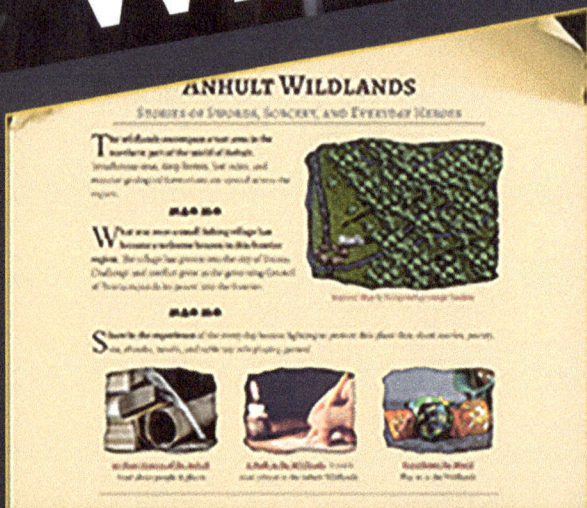

FIRST DRAFT STYLES

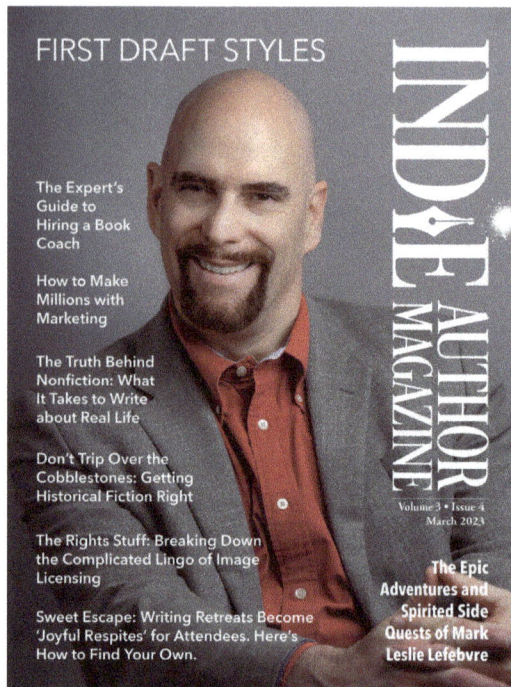

ON THE COVER

REGULAR COLUMNS

THE WRITE LIFE

TYPEWRITER TALES

INDIE
AUTHOR MAGAZINE

EDITORIAL

Publisher | Chelle Honiker

Editor in Chief | Nicole Schroeder

Creative Director | Alice Briggs

Copy Editor | Lisa Thompson

ADVERTISING & MARKETING

Inquiries | Chelle Honiker
publisher@IndieAuthorMagazine.com

Information
https://IndieAuthorMagazine.com/
advertising/

CONTRIBUTORS

Comfort Amaechi, Angela Archer, Elaine Bateman, Victoria Blisse, Patricia Carr, Bradley Charbonneau, Honorée Corder, Jackie Dana, Heather Clement Davis, Jamie Davis, Laurel Decher, Sharon Dooley, Fatima Fayez, Gill Fernley, Greg Fishbone, Jac Harmon, Marion Hermannsen, Steve Higgs, Chrishaun Keller-Hanna, Audrey Hughey, Kasia Lasinska, Monica Leonelle, Jenn Lessmann, Megan Linski-Fox, Craig Martelle, Angie Martin, Kevin McLaughlin, Lasairiona McMaster, Jenn Mitchell, Susan Odev, Tiffany Robinson, Clare Sager, Grace Snoke, Joe Solari, David Viergutz

SUBSCRIPTIONS
https://indieauthormagazine.com/subscribe/

HOW TO READ
https://indieauthormagazine.com/how-to-read/

WHEN WRITING MEANS BUSINESS
IndieAuthorMagazine.com

Athenia Creative | 6820 Apus Dr., Sparks, NV, 89436 USA | 775.298.1925
ISSN 2768-7880 (online)–ISSN 2768-7872 (print)

Design like a Pro for free

FROM THE EDITOR IN CHIEF

Six months ago, I wrote "The End" on the first draft of my current manuscript. It was some time in the early evening, in the middle of the work week. I remember sitting on the floor beside my writing desk and pausing my music to type those final words.

I'll admit it: There were a few tears shed.

Thinking back on it now, it feels like small potatoes when I consider the accomplishments of the authors we feature in these pages—Mark Leslie Lefebvre, this month's featured author, being no exception. I also certainly looked past how much more work there was to do before I would share the story with others. As the second book I've actually finished and the first I felt could be worthy of publishing, I was simply elated to see it complete. As I should've been.

The journey from idea to the finish line is challenging for any author. (If any of you are shaking your heads at that statement, please, share your secrets with the rest of us!) Whether it's your second book or your seventieth, you'll spend any number of hours working on it, in slow-and-steady daily writing sessions or over short stretches of time dedicated only to your story, like in the writing retreats *IAM*'s Audrey Hughey details in this month's issue. You'll wrestle with finicky plot points that don't work the way you want them to and wrestle away from the plot bunnies that show up at the same time. If you struggle with that last one, this month's Mindset article offers some tips.

Writing a first draft is a journey, not just for our characters, but for us too. And finishing that journey deserves to be celebrated every time—happy tears and all.

Nicole Schroeder
Editor in Chief
Indie Author Magazine

Author Outreach

Authoring is a lonely business. It's just you and your computer, pad, phone, or dictation device telling the story that's in your head. The good news is that there are a lot of authors. It's better to be alone together.

How do you find other authors in your genre? Search the books of the type you write. Find those with a comparable number of reviews. And if you haven't published? Look for those authors who are just starting out with one or two books in your genre.

Find them on social media within an author group. Comment and like things they post. Simple. Earn your name recognition, understanding that it takes time. The best thing you can do is watch the other authors' (plural) struggles as they work to find more readers, grow the foundation of their businesses.

You may never have to talk with them as you learn what they've learned. And you'll find that you have things to share, too, on your learning journey. Alone but together. And then you'll find that you probably have a lot in common.

Phrases to avoid: "I'm an author, too!" It doesn't resonate with an established author. This is why it's important to be in author-centric groups. It goes without saying that members are authors. Just like Batman, you shouldn't have to tell people you're Batman. Strangers, yes, but not the person who's ahead of you in their authoring journey.

You should avoid telling them you read their book. It makes for uncomfortable conversations unless it is simple praise. "I love how you integrated the cat and made him such an a**hole. He's just like my cat." That conversation is completely different. It's not fangirling, it's talking about specifics and mechanics of a story. It's a conversation that authors and readers can easily share.

Don't go this alone. Find your fellow authors and ease your way into the fold. As always, keep writing. Nothing like the newest book to shine a light on your other work. ∎

Craig Martelle

Dear Indie Annie,

I write in a genre that is dominated by males: male authors, male main characters. I know my writing is important, but it gets discouraging to know I'm one of the few women in the room. Am I truly making a difference?

Breaking Barriers in British Columbia

Dear BB,

Genderism sucks, doesn't it? There, I said it. Many of us feel confined by the roles and boundaries society, culture, and tradition impose on us because of our gender identities. Male is this; female is that. There are lines we aren't supposed to cross, even in the twenty-first century.

Take my job, for example. In Britain, I would likely be called an agony aunt, never an agony uncle. Perhaps that is simply down to better alliteration, but I suspect the term has stuck because the role grew from advice columns in newspapers and magazines aimed largely at women. Even though the advice may have been penned by a man, such advice was considered more acceptable coming from a woman. That said, in the US and elsewhere, my job would come without any gender bias, being described simply as an advice columnist.

I share this nugget of international trivia to illustrate a point. You are an author, not an authoress. Yes, that word exists, but all the dictionaries I could find when working on this article stated that the term is dated and no longer in use. In fact, as I typed, my editing software put a nice red line underneath the word to alert me to its obsolescence.

Does this mean that men and women, or those who identify as either, can now boldly go where their gender identities have not gone before? Sadly, no. BB, you haven't said what genre you write in, but we all recognize that there are book categories seemingly dominated by one gender or another. However, all may not be as it seems. Many authors hide their true identities behind pen names, often to be accepted in areas where they have concerns about how their real names will be accepted. Some of the most successful

Need help from your favorite Indie Aunt?
Ask Dear Indie Annie a question at
IndieAnnie@indieauthormagazine.com

writers of all time have adopted either gender-neutral names or pseudonyms deliberately designed to mask their gender identity. Have you heard of Mary Ann Evans? Maybe not, but you probably do know the works of George Eliot. Or, to be more contemporary, what about Robert Galbraith? She, of course, is better known in the literary world as J. K. Rowling, though her friends and family probably call her Joanne. And did you know best-selling Historical Romance writer Jennifer Wilde is really a man called Tom Huff? Of course, you may know him better as Edwina Marlow, Beatrice Parker, or Katherine St. Clair.

Does this mean that you have to use a gender-neutral name to succeed in your genre? Not necessarily, but I urge you to consider your personal writing goals. You say that not only is your genre dominated by male authors but also by male characters. I sense from your question that you want to change that. Maybe by giving yourself a gender-neutral pen name, you can infiltrate the genre and influence it positively by providing strong, multi-layered female protagonists. Or are you actually wanting to attract female readers? Where would you find them? How would you market your books to them? Are there allied or alternative subcategories that you can target? Consider how your covers can help convey how your books offer something the same but different, and so on.

Can you change people's expectations or perceptions? Of course you can—with a compelling story and the right marketing.

You may be too young to remember a world before Lara Croft, but believe your aging auntie Indie Annie when I say she really was a game changer (pun intended). Who would have thought that female protagonists could be feisty adventurers too? From zero to hero, such female main characters are now ubiquitous.

Were Lara's creators female? Er, no. But they cracked the glass ceiling that many female writers have pulled themselves through afterward.

Did it matter, back in 1996, that *Tomb Raider* featured a female main character? For the gameplay, probably not, but it made the game stand out in a saturated market. Yes, people can and do argue that Lara was designed to appeal to teenage male fantasies, but she also helped recruit legions of girl players. Her legacy can be felt in successful books like Suzanne Collins' Hunger Games trilogy.

I leave you with this famous quote that Gandhi actually never said (Is anything as it seems?): "Be the change you want to see."

Happy writing,
Indie Annie

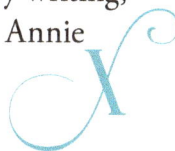

10 TIPS FOR
FACEBOOK GROUPS

More than nineteen years since it launched, Facebook is still the largest social media platform, with three billion users in January 2023, according to DataReportal (https://datareportal.com/essential-facebook-stats). But organic reach on Facebook Pages is declining as paid traffic takes over users' feeds. According to Hootsuite, the average organic Facebook Page post now sees engagement from 0.07 percent of followers. Having a Facebook Group could offer a better way to grow and maintain an engaged community and generate traffic in your favor.

A Facebook Group shouldn't replace your business' Page but can be an addendum for those who desire more exclusive access to a community centered on you and your brand. When creating and managing a Group, it's important to begin with a strategy in mind. Hopefully, the tips below will give you some ideas and insight to get started.

1 ASK WHY, WHAT, AND WHEN

Groups differ from Pages because you control who uses it and how. Once you've decided a Group will meet your business objectives, ask these questions to clarify its purpose and identity:

Why are you creating this Group? Are you an author creating a reader group for your fans? An editor, cover designer, formatter, or other service provider creating a space for your clients? Pinpointing the Group's purpose is an important first step.

What kind of content will I share and/or allow to be shared? How much will you limit posting? Will you allow personal posts, self-promotion, or political or religious posts?

When will you post to the Group and engage with your audience? Consistency is important, as with any social media presence, but it's completely up to you. Browse your favorite authors or service providers to see if they have private Groups and how they're run for ideas.

2 VELVET ROPE OR OPEN ACCESS?

Have you ever tried to get into an exclusive club or party? Remember the feeling of elation when the bouncer lifted that velvet rope for you? This is the feeling your fans have when they ask for access to your private reader group, author group, review crew or street team group, or services group.

Facebook Groups allow you to manage privacy settings, meaning you can make them private. You also have the option to be public, in which anyone can find and join, or secret, where you won't show up in searches and members join on an invite-only basis. This can be done via a link, such as something you might put at the back of your book, or by sending an invitation directly to someone's Facebook profile.

In a public Group, comments, posts, and other engagements are, well, public. Anyone on the internet can view them. In a private Group, however, posts, comments, and anything within the Group are only visible to that Group's members. And if you really want that velvet rope experience, or you want to limit who requests membership, the secret option might be for you.

Pro Tip: You can change your Group's privacy settings at any time.

3 CLARIFY WITH YOUR NAME

If you make your Group private but discoverable, which means anyone can find your Group but not anyone can join, then your name is an important factor to consider.

If your name is Rachel Paige and you want to create a reader group, the simplest, most searchable choice would probably be Rachel Paige's Reader Group, Fans of Rachel Paige Books, or Readers of Author Rachel Paige. Suppose you're creating a private Group for clients or people interested in your work. In that case, you might use something like Rachel Paige Covers, Romance Covers by Rachel Paige, or Rachel Paige Editing Services.

When picking a name, think about the easiest thing someone can type into the search bar to get your Group to show up.

4 MAKE RULES AND ENFORCE THEM

Generally, the rules for a public Group can be more lenient than those for a private Group, but in either case, if you make a rule, you must enforce it. Even if it means kicking your bestie out because they hit their three strikes, you've got to be willing to do it.

Think about Groups in which you've been a member. Do you feel more comfortable in a Group that's lenient with rule enforcement? Or are you more comfortable knowing the rules aren't negotiable?

5 USE THE FEATURED SECTION

Do you have a sale or promotion happening? Book signings for the holidays? Put it in the Featured section. This section allows you to make an initial post about a topic, then pin it where new members can continually see it when they join.

This section is also useful if you have regularly scheduled events. Members can interact with a post without having to scroll to find it. Just create one post that collects comments and mark it as featured. There isn't a limit on the number of posts you can feature, but keep your members' user experience in mind. Fewer featured posts makes searching for something important easier.

6 USE EVENTS WITHIN YOUR GROUP

Create an "Event" within your Group if you're having a meetup, webinar, flash sale, or going live. Like pinned posts, these help to highlight anything important that's happening. It also allows you to reach more members because it automatically shows up in their news feeds. Events in Groups are set up just like on Pages. Find the tab at the top of your Group and follow the instructions to get started.

7 KEEP IT AUTHENTIC AND ON-BRAND

No matter how you use your Group, keep it authentic to you and your brand. Always be yourself—genuine passion and enthusiasm can be engaging and help people connect with you—but decide early on what and how much you will share. If you make rules such as no hate speech, political or religious posts, or bullying, you should also follow them. The downward spiral of online feuding can be ugly and get out of control fast. If you're a professional nurturing a Group, it's best to stay on topic and on brand at all times.

8 USE OTHER PLATFORMS TO DRIVE TRAFFIC TO YOUR GROUP

Do you have a Facebook Page, Instagram, TikTok, website, newsletter, or other online presence? Use that space to drive traffic to your Group. Entice followers with exclusive content or events they can only access from your Facebook Group. Just make sure you give them an easy-to-follow call to action, such as "click here to join," with a link that takes them straight to your Group.

Pro Tip: Use the access request for your Facebook Group to collect email addresses. Facebook allows you to create a series of questions that anyone requesting to join your Group must answer before they're granted access. Here, include one such as: "If you want to receive promotional material and more exclusive goodies from Rachel Paige, enter your email here." Phrasing it like this counts as an opt-in, so you can add this person to your newsletter list. Here's the catch: Whoever is approving memberships has to record that email address before approving the member. Once you hit the Approve button, that email address disappears.

USE AN ADMINISTRATOR (OR TWO!)

**Me: How many words have I written?
Is it a million?
Is it TWO million?**

Word counter: 409 words

Me: LIES!!!

9   Managing a Facebook Group can be time intensive, especially in a large Group with members communicating and sharing through different time zones. Having administrators to monitor incoming posts and comments can be a salvation.

Admins can monitor incoming posts, post on your behalf, answer members' questions, and more. They can be active members who want to volunteer some time to your cause; paid positions, like a virtual assistant; or friends or family members who want to support you. Who you pick is completely up to you. Just make sure the person, or people, you choose understand the rules of the Group and are consistent and reliable.

USE YOUR GROUP TO SELL

Further your Group's velvet-rope experience by inviting members to purchase special, member-ex-

10   clusive merchandise. These could be signed book copies for holiday gifts, bookmarks, pens, author merchandise, or anything else your most loyal fans would love. Post about it in your Group and link to a Google Doc where members can fill out an order form. Collect payment through your preferred provider, and voila! You're taking orders without spending a dime of your own money.

You don't have to "spam" your members, but they're there because they love what you have to offer. When you use your Facebook Group to create a meaningful, engaged community, you have the opportunity to take your audience from fans to superfans. ◼

Tiffany Robinson

The Epic Adventures and Spirited Side Quests of Mark Leslie Lefebvre

Mark Leslie Lefebvre speaks in asides. In telling his story, he meanders about, describing the characters and side quests within the journey. "I've got squirrel tendencies left, right, and center," he explains. However, listening to him wander through stories and back again, one feels as if they have gone on an epic journey through time and space. The thirteen-year-old Lefebvre (pronounced Le-Fave) would be pleased to know he'd achieved this level of storytelling.

Lefebvre is one of the most recognized faces in author circles. As both an independently and traditionally published author, he has been working in the publishing sphere since 1992. At Kobo and Draft2Digital, he has helped bring independent publishing tools to authors while writing his own novels and nonfiction. Lefebvre appears often on podcasts and at author conferences discussing the tools of the trade. He not only writes; he shares what he learns and is passionate about helping others succeed. And don't let that formidable height and striking countenance fool you—there's a big heart lurking behind the smile, ready to help you up the mountain.

WHERE THE STORY STARTS

By the sparkle in his eye, the epic tale of Mark Lefebvre begins with the influential teachers etched in his mind. There is the sixth-grade teacher who didn't just teach but pulled him in to learn. A history and social sciences teacher who told anecdotes and made the past come alive. A math teacher who connected math, physics, and creativity in a tangible concept. The camp leader who told enthralling stories around the campfire. The librarian who hoarded the books Lefebvre needed for his journey.

To honor them, Lefebvre puts them in his stories. "The character in one of my Horror novels was the amalgamation of all the really amazing teachers I've had, plus [the Robin Williams character] John Keating from *Dead Poets Society*." This character must closely resemble Lefebvre too; he—like the character Keating—leads indie authors from the top of the desk, asking us to look at the world differently.

Embodying characters is something Lefebvre learned early on. He jokes that the library was a haven from the bullies chasing him, but he says, "I was all over books like a cheap suit." Around the age of thirteen, the game Dungeons and Dragons (D&D) entered his life. "It was a different form of storytelling. With D&D, everyone was like me." He went from a boy crafting extended stories alone with his figurines to enacting them with a group of other kids. Further empowered by the role-playing and crafting of characters and stories, he began to write his first novel. An Epic Fantasy "of about thirty thousand words," he enacted the fight scenes in his room to be sure he described them accurately. This often led to his mother inquiring what he was up to. "I thought you were writing?" she'd say, overhearing the battles.

To Lefebvre, it is more than just writing, more than just storytelling. "It's interactive storytelling magic," he says. "It's in the head and in the heart." He holds his hand to his head and then over his heart as he speaks, the look in his eyes instantly transporting him to a long-ago epic journey.

A CHARACTER ON STAGE

A self-proclaimed "omnivert," Lefebvre leans toward introversion; in a crowded room at confer-

ences, he heads toward those he knows and lets others approach him for interaction. He prefers playing a role given to him when he's in front of an audience, he says. "In person, I can perform. I'm acting like a confident person. But the minute you put me in the middle of the room, I don't know what to say."

This behavior has its roots in his previous career as a bookseller and experience in theater. When his bookselling career began in 1992, he adapted the confidence of playing a part for customers. A manager once said to him, "You're an actor and you're playing the role of best bookseller ever," before showing Lefebvre the punching bag in the back storeroom for any moments that required it. Lefebvre didn't need it much. He learned that humor is both release and distraction.

"I think this translates beautifully to authors," Lefebvre says. "Your job as an author is to create the most incredible experience for the reader to either escape into your worlds of fiction or to teach them something or inspire them."

This focus on the reader has its roots in Lefebvre's youth. Inspired by Piers Anthony's *Notes to a Reader* at the back of most of his books, Lefebvre leaves his own notes for readers of his work. "And it's really funny," he says with a chuckle, "because I look back at all the notes to a reader and I realize all the things I didn't tell them yet. But that's OK; I'll tell them in future additions." Thinking in marketing terms, he describes the notes to a reader as bonus content—a way for the reader to "understand a bit more about the author and the story, and if they want that, it's there for them, all for the taking."

A gander at Lefebvre's YouTube reveals more about the man: In addition to a healthy dose of helpful videos for authors, there's "Mark's Tavern," a parody of the television show *Cheers*, or playlists like "Spirits Untapped," with videos of haunted hotels and the other type of spirits, as well as "Stark Reflections on Writing and Publishing." We discover dark humor, songwriting skills for parody, poetic musings about whisky, and a flair for the dramatic. Lefebvre finds the delight in life and records it for us. Road trips with his son turn into photo opportunities: Once, when stranded, they took a

Planes Trains and Automobiles photo to not only mark the event but turn what would otherwise be a frustrating day into a father-son memory. Lefebvre is, in many ways, still that thirteen-year-old on an epic journey, inventing, acting, playing, and adventuring. His quest, it seems, is to take the road less traveled and make it his own.

PANDEMICS AND PROCRASTINATION

A self-proclaimed "pantser going down rabbit holes," Lefebvre loves discovery writing and ensures that he hires editors and puts up preorders because "I am motivated by … I guess, fear," he says. When he writes he tries to surprise himself. "What do I want more of?" he asks.

Writing both fiction and nonfiction, he is, at heart, a researcher. "The details are very important to me. The world the characters live in has to make sense in regards to time and space," he says. Researching has an additional benefit: It becomes "a wonderful excuse for procrastination."

Perhaps surprisingly, Romance is one of Lefebvre's favorite genres. "I'm a sucker for a good Romance," he says. "I love a good love story. Like Horror, Romance transcends genre." This isn't surprising to his partner, Liz Anderson, however, who appreciates his propensity for writing daily jokes on a chalkboard outside their home.

"Mark seeks to bring joy and optimism to those he interacts with," she says.

Lefebvre has found his person in Anderson. "I barely do anything for her compared to what she does for me," he says. She is his first reader, and the one he bounces ideas off of. When he decided to take a pay cut when leaving Kobo to write more, she supported his choice 100 percent.

Lefebvre laughs when recalling this story. With that decision, he says he went from no time to write to all the time in the world. Instead of writing for forty hours a week, he found himself filling the time with cat videos. He promptly started work for Draft2Digital (D2D) so he could write again. "Draft2Digital is sometimes ten hours, sometimes eighty hours a week, depending on the schedule," he says. But as he describes it, the structure of his commitment to D2D tames his inner squirrel tendencies.

As for his YouTube channel, Anderson prefers to work behind the camera, but there have been some exceptions. When Lefebvre pitched a certain video during the 2020 lockdown, Anderson loved it, but then she looked at him as if he "had three heads," he says, when he told her, "You know, this is a duet." Evidently, she was convinced; <u>"Stuck In This House Here With You (Music parody of 'Stuck in the Middle with You' by Stealers Wheel)"</u> is available on YouTube, with 7.2 thousand views to date. Become a subscriber if you dare.

LEANING INTO THE FUTURE OF PUBLISHING

Beneath Lefebvre's imposing surface is a man on a mission to help others. It's important to him to answer every question he receives from authors. He describes a training video by the Seattle Fish Market, one in which they ponder, "Are we just selling fish, or are we giving people an experience in their day?"

Lefebvre reflects on that video. "I think about all these interactions we have with people throughout the day. … Why not put a little bit of something extra into it to give them a little bit of something more than just the standard?" He continues, "It's just part of my nature as a storyteller. You want them to lean in."

Lefebvre carries this over to training authors on how to pitch their books, asking them, "What's the lean-in moment? What's that moment when you said something and you see them lean in?"

Lefebvre himself is leaning into the next chapter of his epic story by working on his master of arts in publishing from Western Colorado University. The program is structured to give students an in-depth examination of the publishing industry and upcoming technologies publishers may tap into in the future. Lefebvre views this as an opportunity to advance his skills to better serve others.

"Getting an MA in publishing is more than just a few letters on the end of my name or a piece of academic paper," he says. "It's looking at my more than thirty years of experience working within the industry and seeking a way to learn new things and perhaps re-learn some other things I might have gotten wrong along the way."

Lefebvre's drive is inspired by Neil Peart of the rock band Rush, who often would ask himself, "What is the most excellent thing I can do today?" He also takes inspiration from Michael Connelly's character Harry Bosch, whose mantra is, "Everybody counts or nobody counts."

"I have adapted that into my own life and in the way I try to interact with everybody I encounter," Lefebvre says. "Every single person out there, regardless of their age or experience, has something unique and important that I can either learn from or be inspired by. Losing sight of that would be like losing my muse."

Lefebvre looks forward to expanding his understanding of publishing as it evolves. "At the base and heart of it all is my relentless passion for how storytelling, when done effectively, is fundamentally the bringing together and connecting of at least two individuals." One could argue that Lefebvre has a knack for this.

What does Lefebvre see in the future of indie publishing?

"I believe, like I long have, that the future of publishing itself is going to be more collaborative, and that the future of publishing is going to evolve, grow, and incorporate indie publishing as we know it today. But also new brands, spin-offs, and flavors of indie publishing are going to continue the process of providing more writers, more authors, more creative storytellers new opportunities that we likely can't even properly imagine."

I hope, my dear reader, that this final quote made you lean in. Mark Leslie Lefebvre's adventure is only getting more interesting. ∎

Heather Clement Davis

The Expert's Guide to Hiring a Book Coach

Are you someone looking to master the fundamentals of writing? Or are you struggling to learn the ins and outs of book marketing, preferring to sit on the sidelines while you remain hidden behind your desk? As indie authors, we wear a lot of hats, and there are an incredible number of things to learn in order to run a successful business.

Although writing is often touted as a solitary endeavor, working under another person's guidance can be a tremendous help in enabling an author to achieve their dreams. That is where coaches come in. Coaches help authors with both craft and career, their expertise ranging from novel writing to audience visibility and beyond. If you've exhausted avenues in which you can self-teach writing or business skills, or when you feel stuck at a point in your career and are looking for guidance on where to go next, a coach may be the solution. And as a coach with over eight years of experience helping authors to succeed, my goal is to lay out the guidelines for hiring one and provide you with the knowledge you need so you can make the best choice for your career.

There are two kinds of coaches: book coaches and author coaches. Primarily, book coaches will focus on helping the author write a book to the best of their ability, crafting plot and characters to be exceptional before or during the writing process in order to maximize reader enjoyment. This differs from a developmental editor or a beta reader, who helps polish the book after it's already been written. If the author is writing a nonfiction piece, the book coach will help the author outline and hit on key points in the nonfiction topic. A book coach may also help an author with strategies on how to best market the book after publication.

Author coaches are more focused on the overall career of the client and what the author can do to utilize backlist and branding efficiently in order to gain more readers. Author coaches should take the entire catalog of the author, as well as the history of the author's career, into account as they analyze what will work best for the author's long-term success.

Within these different categories of coaching are coaches with various skill sets and specialities, such as plot outliners, advertising specialists, blurb writers, and more. It is up to the author to determine what type of coach is going to work best for them.

HOW TO CHOOSE A COACH

When hiring a coach, it's important for an author to survey their weaknesses. Begin your search by listing out the ways you wish you could improve, both writing-wise and elsewhere. Have readers been pointing out certain weaknesses in your books that need work, such as characterization, word flow, or plot pacing? Or are you struggling to maintain visibility in the current market and unsure how your ads and newsletter can reach new readers? Are you unaware of the differences between listing your book in Kindle Unlimited or going wide and wish to know what your options are? Or perhaps you're struggling with writing a blurb and would rather pay someone else to do the job than attempt to crank out advertising copy for hours on end.

Coaches can help with all these things. The importance of hiring a coach is to have them strengthen the flaws in your own catalog and business strategy. A coach may specialize in your genre, but it's not always necessary, so long as they have knowledge of the fundamentals. Once you've determined your biggest weaknesses, your next step is to find a coach specializing in your chosen category who works well for you.

ASK AROUND

When hiring a coach, fostering a personal relationship is much more important than having a widely known instructor. If a coach has dozens or even hundreds of clients on their roster, they might not be able to give you the personal time needed to enhance your project. You might struggle to obtain their guidance, no matter how famous their most popular client may be. A lesser-known coach with only a few clients may work best for you.

At the same time, there are authors who advertise themselves as coaches who don't have sufficient experience to be guiding anyone's career. Finding a balance between the two is best; you want someone who will care about your career and make time for your project but has enough industry knowledge to give practical advice.

Asking for coaching recommendations on social media or in forums with authors you trust can be a good place to start. Before hiring a coach, see if they have any podcasts, YouTube or TikTok videos, or free content on what they offer. This will give you an idea of their coaching style, what kind of knowledge they have, and if you'll mesh well together. If you've consumed a lot of their free content and found it helpful for your career, they may be the coach for you.

You can also locate coaches at conventions and meet-ups. Networking is just as important for coaching as it is for connecting with other authors. You never know who quietly offers coaching services alongside their author business. And if you're unsure, ask. Some authors do not have a website or an advertised service for coaching, but they may consider taking another author under their wing and instructing them privately in what they know.

Coaches can be long- or short-term. You can hire a coach for an hour or for months at a time. Someone's guidance over a single thirty-minute telephone call can be more valuable than a multi-week mentorship, if you're getting the right advice.

Coaches also offer classes and courses to help teach a number of people at the same time. If you're wavering on hiring a coach, taking a seminar, class, or course can be a good test for whether the investment into their coaching is right for you.

The main goal is to determine if that coach's energy matches your own. A good coach should be just as excited about their client's success as the client is, and should be driven to help you succeed. If your coach isn't, move on.

TAKE THE ADVICE

Authors who hire coaches sometimes pay their mentor for the knowledge they provide, then fail to implement the advice given—perhaps because they disagree, or because carrying out the tasks suggested by the coach seems overwhelming.

You alone know what is best for your business and your books. If something feels off, then it's okay to disregard a piece of advice a coach can give. But good clients also accept the flaws in their own businesses and work to correct them. If a coach tells you your plot needs to be rewritten, or that your blurb isn't working, or a cover needs updating, it's worth considering, because that could be the missing piece in your business.

It's important to distinguish what your hurt pride and ego are telling you and your intuition. It's acceptable to take the lion's share of your coach's advice and ignore other pieces. But if you're consistently disregarding what your coach has to say, then either that coach is not a good fit or you are not ready to be coached. Being coached can sometimes be a grueling process, and it's up to the author to decide if they can handle the mental pressures of what it requires. Coaches are there to push you to be the best you can be, and to do that, sometimes it means getting uncomfortable. Remind yourself that you are paying this person for their guidance, and if it helps with the longevity of your career, it's worth any temporary discomfort, be it taking out scenes in a manuscript or revising your marketing strategy.

Your coach should strive for your success. Working together with a coach can be one of the greatest decisions of an author's career. And done right, the experience can be fulfilling for both coach and client in a variety of ways. It's all about finding the right fit. ■

Megan Linski-Fox

Sweet Escape

WRITING RETREATS BECOME 'JOYFUL RESPITES' FOR ATTENDEES. HERE'S HOW TO FIND YOUR OWN.

Photo credit: Audrey Hughey

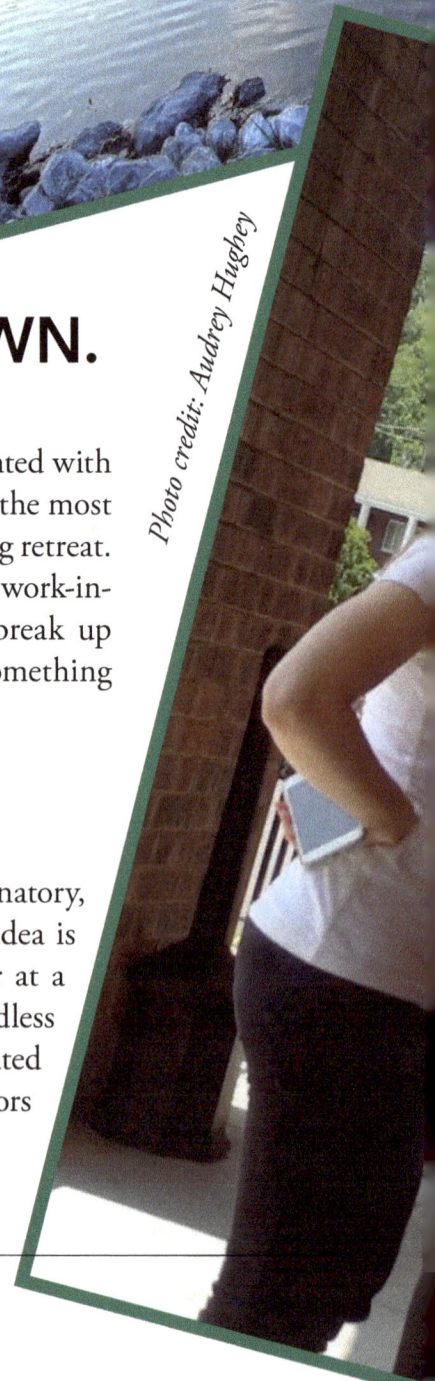

As winter fades and the new year blooms, we're presented with the perfect time to refresh our writing lives. One of the most invigorating ways to achieve that is to attend a writing retreat. Whether you're intending to make a breakthrough on a work-in-progress, connect with your fellow writers, or simply break up the everyday routine, you'll find each experience has something different to offer.

WHAT IS A WRITING RETREAT?

Thankfully, the term "writing retreat" is pretty self-explanatory, but not every retreat is created the same. The primary idea is usually that writers—either as a group or solo—gather at a location away from their homes to write together. Regardless of the particulars, the point of a retreat is to have dedicated time to achieve a burst of progress in your writing endeavors and to reignite your creative spark.

Photo credit: Audrey Hughey

THE BENEFITS OF ATTENDING WRITING RETREATS

Writing retreats can be held over a weekend or last anywhere from several weeks to even a month. The time span is set by the organizer and is usually decided between that person and their inner circle of writing friends or the writing group or organization. Some retreats are only for members of a given organization, but many are open to the public as well. When it comes to location, you can likely find writing retreats that take place in your state or province, or in a place you've always wanted to visit, giving you a dual benefit of traveling. You could stay home if it suits your needs, but you could also travel across your continent or even across the world for a special writing retreat.

Retreats can be homey and affordable, or they can be luxurious and expensive. In one list of 2022 events collected by The Write Life, prices ranged from a couple hundred dollars to multiple thousands of dollars per attendee. Retreats can focus solely on writing, or they can include classes on craft and business, a sort of hybrid between a conference and a retreat. You can even find writing retreats that are themed to intertwine with certain hobbies or exercises, such as yoga and running.

Retreats can include as few as five writing friends renting an Airbnb for a long weekend or as many as several dozen writers. You can also go on a solo retreat if you'd prefer some true

alone time, but it's worth noting many writers already feel alone in their daily lives, so group writing retreats, both in-person and virtual, provide a unique opportunity to feel more connected with kindred spirits.

© NP Designs

Photo credit: Audrey Hughey

"Writing can be a solitary act," says Nan Sampson. "Retreats are joyful respites, providing me with a community of other writers. Together, we learn, share, encourage, and fill the creative well."

The writers you meet at these retreats, friends old and new, are often what make these experiences exceptional and create memories you'll treasure for decades to come.

"It is lovely to be around your people," Allison K. Garcia agrees. "No one looks twice if you talk about your characters as if they were friends or enemies. No one thinks you're weird if you've spent eight hours on deep-dive research about turtles, most of which will never make it into that book. It is lovely to be around your people."

It can also be a chance to spend time with longtime friends that you may not have seen in person for years, like authors N. Terry and J. McCarthy. They had always been friends, writing together since elementary school, but after high school graduation, they hadn't seen each other for a few years until they attended the Author Transformation Alliance (ATA) Spring Writing Retreat in Natural Bridge, Virginia, in 2019.

"The writing retreat meant everything to me," says J. McCarthy. "My favorite part was being with my best friend and other creatives all at the

Photo credit: Nydia Pastoriza

same time. Writing saved my life, and I am so glad I get to do it alongside my favorite people."

Retreats can also change the course of your writing and your life.

"This retreat reignited my love for writing. Everyone there encouraged me and pushed me to pursue a career as an author, something I had given up on as an adult," N. Terry explains. "It was that weekend I started the book I am about to publish. Without going to the retreat, I wouldn't be here now."

Aside from the various social, mental, and emotional benefits that can come with a retreat, you may also find that time away allows you to make massive progress on your manuscript.

Some writers are fantastically disciplined at getting in their needed words, day in and day out, but many others struggle to stay on track when surrounded by the minutiae of life. These weekends can give you the time and space—mentally and physically—to get a giant burst of writing in and catch up on your word count goals.

Even writers who stay on track with their daily and weekly word counts can benefit from attending writing retreats. "As comfortable and utile as my home office is, sometimes I need to get away from the dishes, the laundry, and all the other 'domestic goddess' duties," says P. A. Duncan. "Writing retreats drop me in a 'new world' and

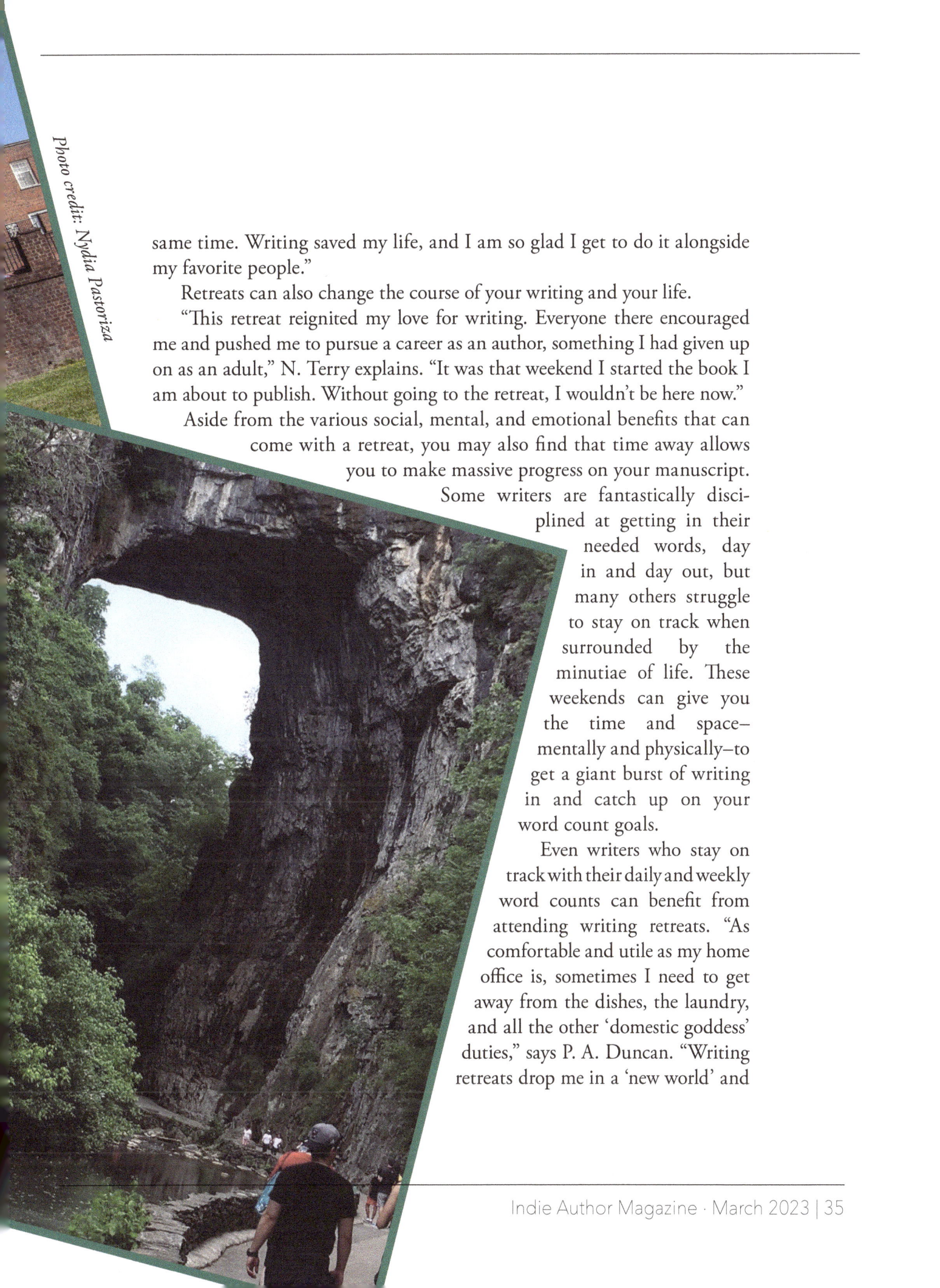

help me approach writing from a different perspective."

WORRIED ABOUT ACCESSIBILITY OR AFFORDABILITY?

If accessibility is a concern, search for retreats that are held at venues meeting your standards and needs. Check the venue's reviews on its website and on Google or travel websites to make sure you feel completely comfortable before committing to the event and buying your ticket.

Photo credit: Nydia Pastoriza

© NP Designs

Many state parks in the United States have risen to the challenge of providing more than meets the bare minimum standards set by the Americans with Disabilities Act. For example, the Natural Bridge Historic Hotel in Virginia provided ample accommodations in 2019 to ensure that all the ATA retreat members could easily navigate the hotel and conference center, and join the group for an excursion via shuttle bus and paved pathways to see the Natural Bridge historic landmark.

Should cost be a major factor for you, don't worry: You can still attend a writing retreat. Although a Google search often nets top results for high-cost events, you don't need to spend a hefty chunk of money to attend a writing retreat you'll love. Ask around in various writing groups and on social media for recommendations for affordable writing retreats—they exist, and they're often best shared through word of mouth.

You could also sign up for a virtual writing retreat in order to save money on travel and lodging expenses yet still connect with other writers who "get it." These virtual events are typically hosted with a website offering a private area for retreat members, a private Facebook group for live connection, and writing sessions hosted over video conferencing software like Zoom.

GETTING STARTED

When searching for a writing retreat, be sure to look several months ahead of when you may want to go, get a clear idea of the time you can take away from your everyday life, your budget, whether you'll choose to travel or stay home, your preferences for group sizes, and your individual needs for accessibility and accommodation.

If you choose to travel, consider the landscapes and scenery that inspire you—or that mirror the setting of your book, if possible. Although some folks love remote state parks and mountaintop resorts, others might prefer the bright lights and buzz of big cities. Should you prefer the latter, remember to balance your love of cities with your writing goals during the weekend. Cities may offer so many activities that you can become distracted from your purpose.

Want to stay home? That's great too! Here are a few simple things you can do to make your home feel like a retreat for a few days:

- Rearrange a space in your home if possible for maximum comfort and to give it a "fresh" feeling.
- Purchase a few small things like scented candles, a throw blanket, a new notebook, and pretty pens.
- Set clear and firm boundaries with your family so you can truly enjoy your at-home retreat.

No matter how you choose to "retreat," set your expectations about what you wish to achieve during that time while staying flexible enough to receive creative inspiration and enjoy the moment to its fullest. ∎

Audrey Hughey

Photo credit: Audrey Hughey

The Truth Behind Nonfiction

WHAT IT TAKES TO WRITE ABOUT REAL LIFE

Although we spend a lot of time talking about fiction—writing to market, craft books, whether you should plot or pants your novel, and more—there is a whole different genre of writing to be considered that can be just as profitable: nonfiction. Like fiction, nonfiction contains many genres that encompass a variety of topics and writing styles specific to those genres.

Nonfiction genres fit into one of four categories, according to Jericho Writers (https://jerichowriters.com): expository, narrative, persuasive, or descriptive. This article and many author craft books are expository nonfiction, written either by experts in the field or researchers who have spent time and effort studying the topic before writing. Narrative nonfiction is any true story about a person, place, or event, including biographies, memoirs, or books covering historic events. Persuasive nonfiction tries to convince you to be for or against an issue—though both sides should be researched and understood before writing starts, and citing references to give your argument credibility is also essential. Finally, descriptive nonfiction uses language that includes the five senses to convey the focus of the book.

Once you know the corresponding category for your nonfiction genre, it will be easier to determine the category, research, and structure you should follow in your own work.

HOW DO YOU FIND AN IDEA?

Idea generation in nonfiction can be as simple as seeing the same topic brought up or question asked repeatedly and knowing a book could bridge the gap in knowledge. It could stem from searching for books on a specific topic and discovering how limited resources are in that area. It could be that you read books on a topic and discover they're out of date, with no one publishing works with the updated information. Are you an expert in your industry or field of work? Do you have a unique philosophy you want to share with others? Have you been part of a world event that you want to talk about? If you answer yes to any of these questions, then you could write about what you know.

If you aren't an expert on a topic, you aren't barred from writing about it, but note that it will take additional time to research the topic in depth and interview those who have expertise to ensure you are credible to your readers. Posts on writing blogs Self-Publisher's Book Plan (https://www.selfpublishersbookplan.com) and JerryJenkins.com include ideas for how to approach the research process and where to find trustworthy information. It might also be beneficial to have an editor who knows about the topic to ensure accuracy in the final version.

Nonfiction books aren't just limited to research topics, how-to guides, or photography. There are plenty of interesting memoirs, biographies, and autobiographies, written after listening to stories passed down by family or friends, after interviewing someone, or based on the author's experiences.

Even when your work is limited by real life, the possibilities for what you write can be endless.

HOW DO YOU KNOW IF THE TOPIC IS SOMETHING PEOPLE WANT TO READ?

One tool that many authors already use to determine categories and keywords for their books can also help at the beginning of the writing process, writes Beth Brombosz on her craft blog, Blogger to Author. Publisher Rocket (https://publisherrocket.com) is a paid program created to help authors review competitors in similar genres to their books, but it can also help nonfiction authors determine potential audiences for their work before they've put pen to page.

By using the keyword search on Publisher Rocket and progressively narrowing search terms from an initial research idea, authors can not only learn how many people are searching for a book on a given topic but also how many competitors they have and what other books have been published already. You may find a topic similar to what you were planning to write has a decent number of people searching for it but very few competitors and decide to go with that angle instead of the one you originally planned.

Also keep in mind questions you see people asking about certain topics repeatedly on social media platforms or forums. If there aren't already books on the topics they're curious about, it may be a sign for you to consider writing one. Knowing there is a potential readership for your book can help direct your work, and you might convince those same people who are asking questions to preorder the book when it's available.

HOW DO YOU STRUCTURE A NONFICTION BOOK?

Much like fiction books, nonfiction books need to have a good flow that leads from section to section and chapter to chapter. But in addition to flow, most nonfiction books have a slightly different structure than fiction books, according to CEM Writing Services (https://cemwritingservices.com). That structure can include:

- Cover
- Dedication

- Table of contents
- Foreword
- Introduction
- Body
- Epilogue or conclusion
- References
- Additional content

The dedication and foreword are optional but typically found in the genre. A foreword should be written by a respected colleague who is knowledgeable about the book's topic. You can't write your own, but though it is not required, including this can boost the credibility of your work to readers.

Alternatively, the introduction should be written by you and include an overview of everything the book covers, as well as why you wrote it. It should sell the book to readers, but it shouldn't leave them with questions in the same way a fiction book's blurb might. Many authors write the introduction after they've written the book itself for this reason.

The body of a nonfiction book can be broken down into chapters, parts and chapters, or another structure, depending on what you are writing. It may be difficult to decide how to structure your book at first; outlining your research and organizing it into logical groupings before you start should help you determine what is best.

Like with the foreword, including a references section is optional, in that some nonfiction books—memoirs, biographies, or some expert-written books—will not need them. In most other cases, however, nonfiction books should include references for any outside resources, research, books, or interviews that you used during the writing process to add credibility and avoid accusations of plagiarism. Be sure to follow the *Chicago Manual of Style* for how to cite references.

Following the references section in your book, you may also choose to include additional content. As in fiction novels, this could be author notes, a call for newsletter sign-ups, a list of other books you've written, and any other back-of-the-book pages you typically create. Although it isn't necessary to prepare these during the drafting process, it can be helpful to know ahead of time which pages you'd like to include so you can record ideas for your author's note or acknowledgements page as you write.

WHAT IS THE WRITING PROCESS LIKE?

Except for memoirs, biographies, and autobiographies, nonfiction should be written with you, as the narrator, addressing the reader. As you would with fiction, pick the tone of voice you want for your book and keep it consistent. Nonfiction can have a fairly casual tone and still be informative, writes Boni Wagner-Stafford in a 2019 article for IngramSpark; you don't have to write it like a college paper, unless the topic is targeting that audience.

Pro Tip: Maintaining your voice can be difficult if you start and stop writing, but an editor can help adjust your voice to be consistent down the road.

Even if you research your topic beforehand to help with writing, know that you may need to interrupt the drafting process multiple times to research further and prevent inaccuracies. This is especially true when writing a biography or ghost-writing a memoir for an individual. People's memories aren't always accurate, and making sure you have the correct spelling for names and locations or descriptions of where things were as you go helps ensure the accuracy of the product you're creating.

It is important, too, to consider your audience and their level of knowledge on the topic you are writing. This will help guide you in what context you need to include as you write and the academic grade level you should write for.

Here are some other important things to remember, particularly when writing expository or persuasive nonfiction:

- Avoid abbreviations if possible. If you are going to use an abbreviation, spell it out the first time and put the abbreviation in parentheses afterward. Acronyms and abbreviations can change or be lost over time, and taking these extra steps ensures clarity for your reader.

- If necessary, provide a glossary of terms at the back of your book.
- Keep track of where you use reference materials and quotes so you can add them into the paperback version of your book on the appropriate pages, as well as in the bibliography of your book.

IS IT POSSIBLE TO "PANTS" A NONFICTION FIRST DRAFT?

Some authors feel it is a mistake to write a nonfiction book without an outline because it will take you longer to write it without set points to discuss, laid out in a specific order in which to proceed. Although it can take hours, or sometimes even days, to complete a nonfiction book outline, it may save you time when you write it and ensure you don't forget certain concepts.

Of course, just like with fiction, as you write your nonfiction book, you will recognize parts you may have missed when creating your outline and be able to add to your book as you go. But an outline, even if it's just an overview, will make it easier for you to write the book and keep things organized, according to Wagner-Stafford. If your book has references, knowing where those references will be added and where to include them in the bibliography will also be helpful. In some cases, your outline may even become your table of contents.

It isn't impossible to "pants" a nonfiction book, but it might be easier to have your outline and research done ahead of time. There are a variety of ways to outline a nonfiction book and though some of it depends on what you are writing, the rest depends on how in-depth you like your outlines. Check out these sites that provide a variety of outlines to find the one that best works for you:

- Scribe Media offers a free template with its blog post, "The Simple Way To Outline A Nonfiction Book."
- For memoir writers, Creativindie's "How to write a nonfiction book or memoir" offers outlining templates to help divide your book into recognizable chapters and story beats, much like those found in fiction.
- Cascadia Author Services offers seven outlining options for nonfiction authors to choose from in a 2019 post by Bennett R. Coles (https://cascadiaauthorservices.com/book-structure-template). ∎

Grace Snoke

Back to Basics

HOW WRITERS CAN MAKE THE MOST OF GOOGLE DOCS AND MICROSOFT WORD

Indie authors are in a unique position in the publishing world. We get to make all the decisions when writing and publishing our stories. It's liberating, thrilling, and sometimes a little overwhelming.

Software like Scrivener and Dabble, and programs like Reedsy Book Editor and Atticus, which were designed specifically for authors, provide features that guide writers from planning to publication. These comprehensive tools can organize all of your material, edit it, and get it formatted for print.

Here's a quick overview of a few popular writing platforms:

- **Scrivener**: Great for project management, structure, and productivity. Has a learning curve that may be intimidating. *($59.99 for Windows or MacOS, $23.99 for iOS)*

- **Dabble**: Similar features to Scrivener, but more user-friendly. Subscription pricing is limiting, and does not provide formatting options. *(Three pricing levels from $10–$20/ month)*
- **Reedsy Book Editor:** Free to use and web-based, so it's accessible anywhere, but some authors find formatting challenging, especially for maps and other extra content.
- **Atticus**: Another web-based, all-in-one option. A little pricey, and still working out some bugs, according to Joe Bunting's blog post on *The Write Practice* (https://thewritepractice.com/best-book-writing-software). *($147)*
- **Vellum**: By many accounts, Vellum's formatting is beautiful, but it's expensive and currently limited to Mac users. *($199 for e-book generation; $249 for paperback formatting)*
- **Ulysses**: Limited customization makes it mostly distraction-free, but it wasn't designed specifically for books, and it's only available for Mac users. *($5.99/month)*

Reedsy also recently compared some of the biggest contenders in more depth on its blog. Visit https://blog.reedsy.com/novel-writing-software to read more.

THE CASE FOR KEEPING IT SIMPLE

With so many products and services to choose from at every step of the process, it's easy to forget that the most important part of publishing your novel is to get it written.

For authors who want to focus on the story first and publishing second, tried-and-true word processors may be the answer. Although working within the limits of Google Docs or Microsoft Word can be challenging for some plotters, especially those who don't write chronologically, other authors may find the simplest programs are ideal for drafting, collaborating, and editing.

And because Docs and Word were designed for a wide audience, they both have features you might not expect in a basic writing program.

BENEFITS AND CHALLENGES OF GOOGLE DOCS

Google Docs is popular because of its accessibility—it's free for both Mac and PC, available on any device, and can be used on- or offline—and the relative ease of collaboration. It's great for working with critique partners and sharing with beta readers, although longer documents may experience lagging. "Suggestion Mode" is basically the same as Word's Track Changes feature, which is useful if you're taking advantage of one of Google Docs' best features: autosave. The platform continuously backs up your work as you go, but you don't lose access to those earlier versions, so you don't need to keep multiple draft copies.

Using folders in the Drive to organize research and planning materials can give users an experience that mimics the binder settings in Scrivener and other author-centric softwares. This is especially true if you make use of the seamless integration with other Google apps, like Jamboard and Google Sheets. Docs also allows you to export to Word if your editor or formatting program requires it. Author Sophia Alves is so confident in Google Docs, she uses it for everything from her series outline to working with her agent and preparing for formatting with Vellum and Draft2Digital. Still, writers whose work requires formatting earlier in the process, like poetry and nonfiction, may find Google Docs capabilities somewhat limited in the early stages.

Pro Tip: Google Docs now has a built-in outline, which you access by clicking View > Show Outline. Any headings you add to your document will show up on the left. This can be great for organizing your manuscript or developing a book bible to track characters, settings, and other significant details. Pair this with the document search or bookmark function, and simplify navigation.

Eva Deverell created a PDF and video that go into extensive details on how writers can use Docs to create a workflow, engage with readers, and collaborate with editors in her blog post, "The Ultimate Guide to Google Docs for Writers" (https://eadeverell.com/google-docs). She also has ideas for creating community through live writing sessions where readers can view her manuscript as she writes it. By announcing her live writing sessions on Twitter and through her newsletter, she makes use of the program's chat feature to create an open dialogue with readers. Since you can limit how broadly you share your Doc and whether you give readers access to commenting, this experience for readers is one other authors who use the platform could consider offering as a Patreon reward or newsletter magnet.

BENEFITS AND CHALLENGES OF MS WORD

Word has been an industry standard for several decades for a reason. It's compatible with most other software, it provides a user-friendly Track Changes feature, and its macros make formatting significantly easier. Microsoft Word is also the preferred platform for many editors and publishers, so in some cases, writers may be better off starting their draft there. Editor Jaime Ford Watson says it has "all the features of Google Docs, but with professional level software."

Pro Tip: Using Headings and other Styles options gives you the same navigability as the outline in Docs. The Review tab also offers lots of useful editing functions, including a Read Aloud feature.

Because of Word's small file sizes, sharing is almost as easy as Docs, and it integrates with plug-ins like ProWritingAid for more features. Unfortunately, it doesn't play well with Apple platforms, and switching between Pages and Word can be frustrating. Also, updates and upgrades are not free. If you want to use Microsoft Word online, you need a subscription to Office 365, where 1 TB of cloud storage is going to cost you $6.99 per month or $69.99 per year.

Pro Tip: Try the Readability feature if you have concerns about the overall reading level of your text. Most writing for the general public is expected to be around the fifth grade level, according to The Writers For Hire, though reading levels vary widely by genre and audience.

Find additional details about these and other platforms in Joe Bunting's blog post on *The Write Practice* (https://thewritepractice.com/best-book-writing-software/).

RECOMMENDED PRACTICES FOR BOTH PLATFORMS

- Edit your document's personal dictionary to include any words you want spell check to ignore.
- Both Word and Docs have dictation features. After turning on your microphone in System Preferences or the Control Panel, Google Docs users can find Voice Typing in the Tools menu. MS Word users will find Dictate with a microphone icon in the Home menu. Both work best if you speak clearly, using short pauses between phrases, but you shouldn't need to worry about speaking at your natural rate. Word even made the top five in a list of the best dictation software of 2023 by Techradar.com (https://www.techradar.com/best/dictation-software). That said, neither lives up to the functionality or customization of

a dedicated dictation software, like Dragon *($200 for the Home edition/$150 for the mobile version)*.

- Before you upgrade to a dedicated author software, check out extensions and add-ons that might get you the same features in a word processor you already have. For example, Grammarly offers both a Chrome extension, for use with Google Docs, and a Word plug-in.

WHICH IS RIGHT FOR YOU?

This might sound like a cheat, but you really can have it all.

Although writers have a tendency to find one process and maintain an intense loyalty to it, these different tools offer enough of the same features that choosing one to get you through your entire writing journey isn't strictly necessary. You may find that your preference changes depending on the project, or even the step within the project.

Whether you prefer the consistency of a single program that does it all or benefit from shifting to different software as you work through your process, keep Google Docs and MS Word in mind. The basics have come a long way, and you might find that they have exactly what you need. ■

Jenn Lessmann

Tech Tools

Courtesy of IndieAuthorTools.com
Got a tool you love and want to share with us?
Submit a tool at IndieAuthorTools.com

CAMPFIRE WRITING

CampfireWriting.com is a website that offers online writing courses and coaching services for aspiring writers who want to improve their skills and achieve their writing goals. The website was founded by Emily Gould and Leah Beckmann, who are both experienced writers and editors with a passion for helping others develop their writing talents.

ONE STOP FOR WRITERS

One Stop for Writers is an online platform designed for writers, providing a range of tools and resources to help them with various aspects of the writing process. The website was created by Angela Ackerman and Becca Puglisi, who are both bestselling authors and experienced writing coaches.
OneStopForWriters.com

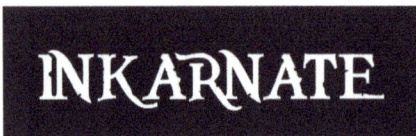

INKARNATE

Inkarnate is an online map-making tool that allows users to create high-quality, customizable maps for a wide range of purposes. The platform was designed to provide an easy-to-use and affordable solution for game developers, writers, and other creatives who need to create maps for their projects.
Inkarnate.com

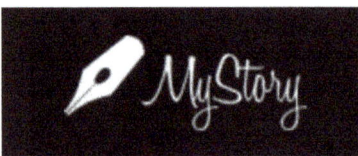

MY STORY TODAY

MyStory.today is an online platform designed to help users create and share their life stories in a unique and engaging way. The website offers a range of tools and resources to help users develop their stories, including writing prompts, photo prompts, and memory exercises.

SPRINGHOLE

Springhole.net is a website that offers a wealth of resources and tools for writers, storytellers, and creatives. The site was created by a team of writers and artists who are passionate about helping others develop their creative talents.

The Rights Stuff

BREAKING DOWN THE COMPLICATED LINGO OF IMAGE LICENSING

Authors need images for many purposes, including book covers, graphics, website images, printed marketing materials, and physical products. But just as your stories are copyrighted, images are copyrighted too, with a host of complex licensing that could trip you up. There are also companies that make a living from finding instances where images have been used without permission. To borrow a line from Liam Neeson's character in *Taken*, they will look for you, they will find you, and while they won't kill you, they will send you a huge fine or even take you to court, where you could get jail time.

So knowing the rights you have to an image is essential, as is understanding what various image licenses mean. However, there are ways to find images with clear licensing terms, so it's easier to find what you want and use it for the right purposes.

WHAT TO CONSIDER WHEN USING IMAGES

When searching for images to use, it can seem like there are as many stipulations for use as there are images on the internet. Every stock site, artist, and photographer will have their own licensing terms you'll need to adhere to. You can usually find these terms on the image listing itself or often in the site's footer. Language varies, but look for wording such as "Licensing," "Terms and Conditions," "How it Works," or similar. Failing that, contact the help desk or the photographer or artist directly to confirm terms. Check what you can do with each image, then check again before you use it.

Be aware that even using an image on your author website, blog, newsletter, or social media is commercial use. It's not just about if you're directly making money from using the image. Also note that "images" means both photos and artistic works, as well as any graphs, charts, and other graphics you didn't create.

How many copies can you use?

Sometimes, it's not just about what permissions you have for a photograph. Some sites limit how many times you can use a particular image. If you're thinking of using an image for your cover or for swag, you could find yourself in a position where you only have permission to use 5,000 copies of that image. Sell more than that, and you'd have to buy another license for that image, and again each time you reach the next 5,000-copy limit. There's also no saying the price won't go up. If you're not careful, you could set yourself up for an admin nightmare.

Assume nothing.

You can't license an image commercially for your cover and assume you can also use it to create physical products, such as mugs, tote bags, or T-shirts. Some-

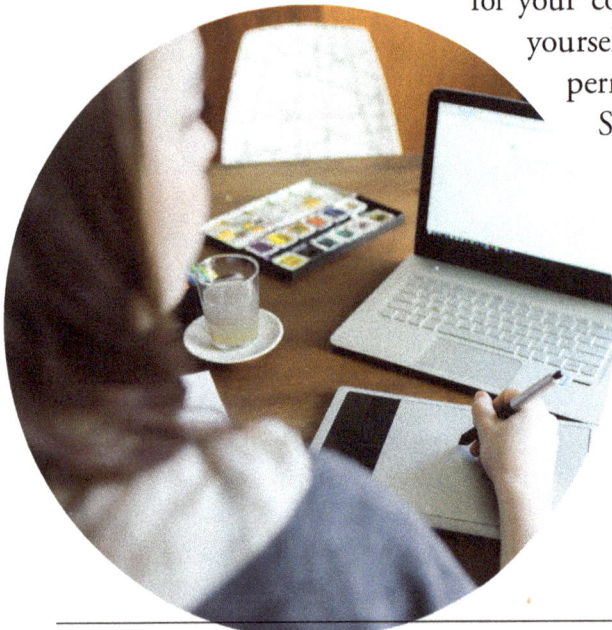

times that's allowed, but usually you'll need to pay for an extended commercial license for product creation. If your cover designer bought the image and you want them to create anything else for you, check whether they've bought the right license, as you may need to pay extra. If they bought the cover image but you want to create items from it, you will also need to buy the image, with the right license, before you can use it. Check license terms or contact the site, photographer, or artist if you want to use an image in ways that weren't addressed in your initial agreement.

You aren't the only one who can buy stock photos.

Unless you paid for an exclusive-use license for an image, anyone may buy the same image from a stock photo site or a photographer and use it on their work too. Unless they've used it in the exact same way, with the same or very similar design elements, they are not copying you, and you can't expect them to take their book down or replace the cover.

IMAGE LICENSES

It would be far simpler if there were just one type of image license, but that's not the case. Here are the main license types and what you can do with them.

Royalty-Free

A royalty-free license means you can buy the rights to an image from a site or photographer for a one-time fee. Unless there are any other restrictions listed, the only things you can't do with that image are claim that you created it and resell it. This is one of the most straightforward licenses, where you can use an image, add to it, or manipulate it without violating copyright.

Creative Commons

Photographers and other creators can also release their work with a Creative Commons (CC) license (https://creativecommons.org/about/cclicenses). With this, the image creator can specify what you're allowed to do with the image based on its license category. There are four main Creative Commons categories that can allow an image to be used commercially:

- With an Attribution license (CC BY), you can make new and different works from the original image and distribute it, as long as you credit the original creator.
- With an Attribution—ShareAlike No Derivatives license (CC BY-ND), you can distribute an image with credit to the creator, but you are not allowed to change it.
- With the Attribution—ShareAlike license (CC BY-SA), you can make new and different works from the original image, but you must credit the creator and issue the new work with the same license that the creator set.

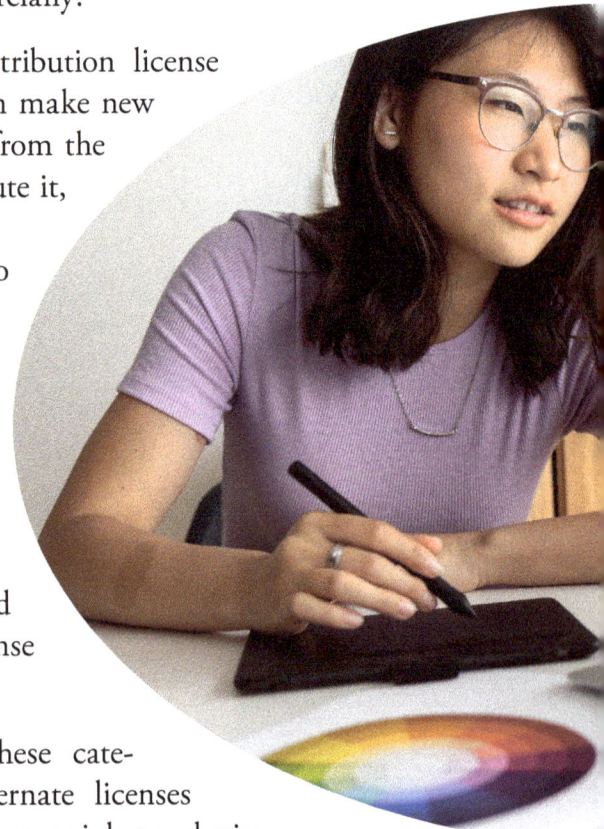

Additionally, these categories have alternate licenses that offer the same rights and stipulations but only allow for non-commercial use. If your image carries a Creative Commons license, pay close attention to whether it includes an "NC," or non-commercial, designation.

If an image is in the public domain (CC0), either it was never copyrighted to begin with or the copyright has expired. In some cases, creators also put their images into the public domain. You

can use these images without permission and without payment, and you don't need to cite where you got the image or give any credit, though attribution is typical.

Pro Tip: Many sites allow you to filter search results based on the specific licensing you're looking for. This is helpful, as you can filter out anything that can't be used commercially.

Rights-Managed Images

Similarly to royalty-free images, with rights-managed images, you can pay a site or photographer once to use their image. However, they are likely to specify how you can use the image, where you can use it, when, and what sizes you can use. Images with this license are more likely to be found on individual photographer and artist sites, as many want control over how their work is used.

Pro Tip: Save money by being clear and narrow about what you want the image for. The more uses and sizes you ask for, the more you'll pay. You can always ask to increase usage later if you need it.

WHERE TO FIND IMAGES

Here are just some sites where you can find quality images with clear licensing:

Depositphotos (https://depositphotos.com)
Depositphotos is a royalty-free site for stock images, videos, and music. Look for deals throughout the year that offer a hundred images for a single payment. We've seen everything from one hundred dollars for one hundred images down to thirty-five

dollars for one hundred images if you buy via AppSumo (https://appsumo.com).

In addition, Depositphotos provides you with a PDF for each image showing your name and what you've bought, which is perfect for proving you have the right to use that image if you are asked.

Creative Fabrica (https://creativefabrica.com)

This site offers a cornucopia of fonts, embroidery, crafts, and graphics. Even better, they have just one license that applies across the site, so you don't need to check individual image licenses. And the site's help desk is responsive if you still have questions.

CreateHER Stock (https://createherstock.com)

This site solely focuses on royalty-free stock images of black women. Contact the site if you want to use their images for commercial use, as you will need to buy an extended license.

Also be aware of this caveat in their license terms: "All users acknowledge that CreateHER Stock and its Contributors do not make any representations or assurances of non-infringement and does not make claim to have received releases from any brands, designers, or manufacturers for use of products, registered trademarks, logos or intellectual property that may or may not be portrayed in images found on this platform."

It may be best to only use images without products and brand logos from this site.

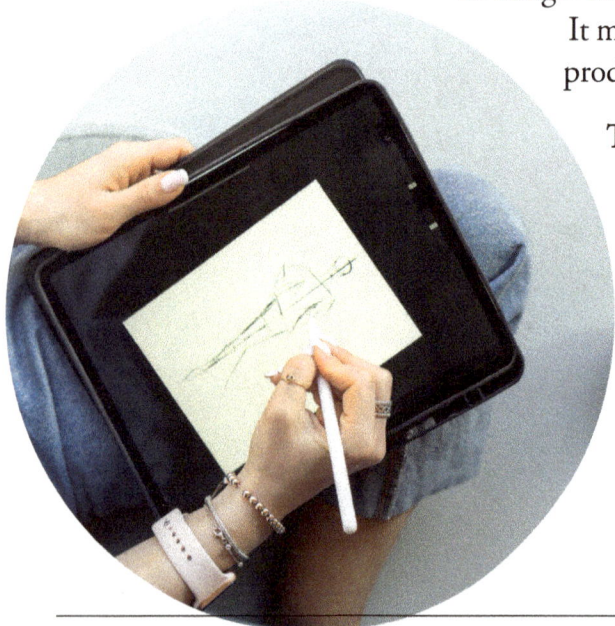

The Killion Group (previously Hot Damn Stock) (https://thekilliongroupimages.com)

Run by authors, The Killion Group carries stock images specifically tailored to Romance books of every subgenre. Photos in its royalty-free library include historical figures, paranormal elements, poses that are a little … hotter, and more.

You can also find Creative Commons images on sites like Flickr (https://flickr.com/creativecommons), and some museums and other companies, like the Metropolitan Museum of Art and NASA, offer selections of their own images for use, though of course, check their licensing.

HOW TO MAKE SURE YOU ARE LEGALLY USING IMAGES

- Use reputable image sites.
- Take your own photos or create your own artwork—then you own the copyright and can use or alter them however you wish.
- Buy images directly from a photographer or artist.
- Find out who owns the copyright on the image you want and ask permission.
- When using images on your website, blog, on social media, or in your newsletter, instead of using an image or embedding it, link to the image and credit the copyright holder. It might not look as pretty, but you will be on the right side of the copyright holder.
- Check what your license says and make sure you have permission for what you want.

No matter how you're using images in your book business, it's imperative you do your own research and check an image's license and any terms and conditions for its use—even on a site you've used previously. And if you're not sure, it's always worth reaching out to the copyright holder to clarify what you can do. Better to have permission than to face a huge fine and potential court case. ■

Gill Fernley

Podcasts We Love

All the Kissing

All the Kissing is a podcast that focuses on the craft of writing romance novels. The podcast features in-depth discussions on topics such as character development, plot structure, and world-building, all from the perspective of the romance genre. The hosts and guests of the podcast are all experienced romance authors, so listeners can be assured that they are receiving expert advice and insights.
https://player.fm/series/all-the-kissing

1st Draft With Sarah Ennie

1st Draft with Sarah Ennie is a podcast that focuses on the craft of writing and storytelling. The podcast features in-depth interviews with a variety of authors and industry professionals, who share their insights and experiences on everything from drafting and revising to publishing and marketing.
https://www.firstdraftpod.com/

The Manuscript Academy

The Manuscript Academy Podcast is an extension of the Manuscript Academy platform, providing valuable insights, interviews, and advice on the writing and publishing process. Hosted by literary agents Julie Kingsley and Jessica Sinsheimer, the podcast features a range of guests, including authors, editors, and other industry professionals.
https://manuscriptacademy.com/podcast

The Truth about Writing Trans Characters

SHOULD YOU WRITE A TRANSGENDER CHARACTER IF YOU DON'T IDENTIFY THE SAME WAY?

In 2017, the Cooperative Children's Book Center (https://ccbc.education.wisc.edu) included LGBTQ+ content in its diversity data collection for the first time. Of the approximately 3,700 books it received that year, only 136 had significant LGBTQ+ content. Of this, four books had a trans primary character. Yet in 2022, there were around 1.6 million Americans who identified as transgender, according to data published by the UCLA. That doesn't seem very representative, does it?

The first fictional work including trans stories is generally held to be *Metamorphoses* by Ovid, so there's no excuse for modern day writers not to include transgender people in their works. Or is there? Cisgender people, or those who identify as the sex they were assigned at birth, might worry that they don't have the knowledge and experience needed to write a character whose body doesn't represent their real gender. These anxieties are valid, but if authors never wrote outside of their experience, we'd probably not have fiction at all.

So is it okay for cisgender writers to write trans characters? For trans author Ela Bambust, it's not only okay; it's important for them to do so. "Maybe don't make them [a trans character] the main character without co-writing with a trans person, because you're likely to get a lot about the lived experiences wrong if you don't," she writes, "but trans people are a part of life and they deserve to be present in cis-created media."

Your character's transness should add to their identity—just having a character who explicitly introduces themself as trans helps no one, Bambust writes. "Instead, just have a character who others refer to with they/them, someone who's trying a new name, or whose core theme is already transformative and a bit transgressive."

HOW CAN CIS WRITERS SENSITIVELY RESEARCH TRANS CHARACTERS?

Conversations with actual trans folk about their lives and experiences are the best way to write realistic trans characters. Talk to trans people first, before you even start writing your story ideally, though using the internet is a valid way to look up information too. Websites such as The National Center for Transgender Equality (https://transequality.org) and the Gay & Lesbian Alliance Against Defamation's (GLAAD) transgender resources are good places to start. Make time for trans beta readers or sensitivity readers at the end of your writing process as well, so you can avoid accidentally upsetting your readers with any stereotypes and tropes you might not recognize are problematic, such as the sexually aggressive trans person or the trans person who only exists to be a point of crisis for a story.

WHAT GENRES ALLOW FOR TRANS CHARACTERS' STORIES?

Transgender characters can fit into any genre, but Bambust says she'd especially like to see more trans characters in Sci-Fi, Fantasy, and Romantic Comedy, especially in roles that don't focus on them being rejected by friends and families, on their surgeries, or on triggering topics like suicide. A lot of fiction revolves around the challenges and hardships of being trans, but that is only a fraction of their experiences. Avoid using a character's transness as the only conflict point in your writing, and balance out these moments with joy-filled happenings too.

Bambust's biggest piece of advice to cis writers is to represent a community and not just a single person.

"A single trans woman in a cast of cis people is extremely unrealistic. Trans people flock together," she writes. "If you have just the one, that token character has to be the face of the community, and it forces you to either make them as bland as possible to avoid stereotypes—in which case, why make them trans for any reason other than tokenisation? Or you have to make them a programmer with knee-high socks and a blåhaj [a toy sold by IKEA that's become a recognized symbol in the LGBTQ+ community] who has two girlfriends and blue hair and a nose piercing so people can definitely know she's trans."

She continues, "Having several trans characters allows you to acknowledge the trans community as a community, and allow for a degree of subtlety in their characterisations."

Don't let your concerns hold you back from writing the fiction you want to write, ask questions, and be sensitive to the communities you're representing in your writing. Most of all, embrace the fact that your cis-centric view of the world isn't the only one, and you'll be on your way to writing trans stories that every reader will love. ■

Victoria Blisse

Don't Trip on the Cobblestones

So you have decided to write a historical novel. Were you impressed by the fifty-year scope in Amor Towles' *A Gentleman in Moscow*? Or perhaps you were intrigued by the spy craft in *The Rose Code* by Kate Quinn? Historical Fiction is expansive, stretching across time periods and crossing paths with several other genres. Its variety makes it popular among readers, but it also can make for a more exciting experience for authors as well. So where does one begin?

First, one must meet the definition of a novel in this genre. Typically, Historical Fiction should depict events from over fifty years ago that are set in an actual time and place, according to Celadon Books. Cole Salao of TCK Publishing further describes Historical Fiction as "blending the real and the imaginary." There can be exceptions with Romance, Historical Sci-Fi, Mystery, or Fantasy set in recognizable societies, of course.

Historical Fiction began in the early nineteenth century and remains popular today. Even though World War II ended in 1945, novels about the war, such as *All the Light We Cannot See* by Anthony Doerr, and *The Nightingale* by Kristin Hannah, remain top sellers. Yet another recent book, *Sisters of the Great War* by Suzanne Feldman, is set around World War I, over one hundred years ago.

No matter which time period you choose, every Historical Fiction—in every time period—needs to get the basics of the genre right in order to succeed with readers. That means mastering particular story elements early on to define your story's base, create depth, and enrich your story world overall.

GETTING HISTORICAL FICTION RIGHT

DEFINE YOUR BASE: PERIOD, SETTING, AND SOCIAL ISSUES

Once you've chosen your genre, establish your book's historical period and setting. Is the story set in regency England, the antebellum South, or during World War II? Each of these settings has particular historical facts that require research to establish authenticity.

Research your chosen time period well and look for source materials long before you write. Use movies you've watched that impressed you and the historical books you enjoyed from the time. Also consider social mores, especially for women, during period stories. What habits were taboo, such as public drinking or smoking, for a lady in the nineteenth century? How do enslaved people, minorities, or gay people interact with your characters? Is there travel between "then" and "now" as in the Historical Fiction Mystery *The Lost Apothecary* by Sarah Penner? If so, consider how the answers to these questions might conflict for certain characters.

CREATE DEPTH: CHARACTERS, CONFLICT, DIALOGUE, AND THEME

In all fiction, authors must create powerful characters, accurate dialogue, and devise a theme. Will you be using the trope of forced marriage to save a family fortune? Or that of righting wrongs, such as the abolitionist or suffrage movements? Each of these topics brings you a chance to explore another important area in the genre: that of historically correct conflict for your protagonist.

On a smaller scale, your dialogue should also match the time period you've chosen for your book. Be sure your characters use phrases common to the time, such as using "swell" during a World War II novel or "cat's pajamas" when writing about the roaring twenties.

ESTABLISH AND ENRICH YOUR FICTION: WORLD-BUILDING

Recall a city street scene in any recent movie and think of the extras hawking their wares or the cab horns blaring. Here the director is showing you the cacophony of the city. When world-building, show scenes of chaos or serenity with vivid descriptions; your reader needs to appreciate the surroundings as you depict another dimension.

What were the streets like in your story's chosen time period? Were they smelly and muddy, strewn with manure from the many horse-drawn carriages common before the automobile? Or did they have cobblestone pavements? How were homes built and heated? Did industrial pollution cover the city with acrid smoke?

When asked if she visited the battle sites for her book about World War I, author Suzanne Feldman laughed and said she had learned her lesson when writing a previous book. She had traveled to the deep South to see certain sites described in it, but the trip was long and tedious; she got lost and had to call for directions. For her most recent book, she says, she used Google Maps, as well as an original surgical nurse's diary to add details to her hospital fiction.

Meanwhile, for her book, Sarah Penner reviewed old maps of London and descriptions of potions from two hundred years ago to make her storylines work, according to a 2021 Q&A with Heather Caliendo for Book Club Chat. Real-time diaries and memoirs can add color to your scenes as well.

How your characters dress matters too. You cannot give a character a wristwatch before they were in common use, for example. (Artisans made the first one for the Queen of Naples in 1810.) Did women's dresses have bustles? Did men wear wigs?

Tropes are common in all kinds of story-telling and can be great for world-building. We know the common ones: the good guy wears the White Hat; the bad guy, the Black Hat. But it is best to consider them carefully—including which harmful ones to avoid, writes ProWritingAid blog manager Krystal N. Craiker. (Surgical nurses belied the trope that women fainted upon seeing blood, for example.)

Whatever—and whenever—your story, be sure to build your characters' world before you write to ensure your reader will have the best experience.

Writing for ProwritingAid.com, Krystal N. Craiker notes that the winners often wrote history. Therefore, the white savior rides in on his white horse in the European version of history, but in reality, the world is diverse and the savage tribe is not the norm, no matter the continent on which one lives. It is best to avoid using the following tropes, which can include harmful descriptions and stereotypes.

- The **white savior trope** perpetuates the idea that people of color are weak and need saving.
- The **savage tribe** adds to the idea that natives of any country are not to be trusted.
- The **damsel in distress** continues the stereotype that women are weak and need a man to rescue them.
- The **dark-skinned villain**, much the same as the savage tribe, equates dark skin with bad characters.
- The **tragic queer love story** ignores the actual presence of queer people in the world and inserts moral judgments on their character; authors should allow them happy endings.
- The **faceless, nameless token character** is used to show diversity but does not give them a real function. ■

Sharon Kay Dooley

If at First You Don't Succeed, Write, Write Again!

Staring at a blank cursor can be even more stressful than staring at a low bank account balance.

But as someone very wise once said, you can't edit a blank page.

I like to think about the words I write as money seeds I'm planting—I just have to patiently (okay, sometimes impatiently) wait for them to grow into money trees.

The good news, and I only like to share good news, is you can close your eyes—it's easier to not see a blinking cursor with your eyes closed—and let the words flow through your fingertips.

It's a challenge, I know, to write something that "isn't perfect" (yet) or that we know needs a ton of work before it's ready for the eyes of others.

Keep in mind every author must go through rounds of revisions after they complete their first draft. Every single author. My books go through a dozen rounds of review before I release them to the public.

Your first draft may not resemble your final draft—maybe not even a little. My most recent manuscript had eight different versions, each one growing, changing, and rearranging! The final draft, a.k.a. *the book*, hardly resembles what I started with.

Do you need to hear that I've written hundreds of thousands of words (read: seeds) that have yet to turn into money trees? Well, I have! But because I keep at it, keep refining my process, working on my writing, and marketing, and monetizing, and I don't let any grass grow under my feet, I exponentially increase the likelihood my first drafts will turn into best earning books.

Plenty of people have written, and I'm sure many more will tackle the subject, about writing one's first draft. Perhaps my point of view can add some perspective and hope all at the same time. Here is what I keep in mind when I'm working on a project's first draft:

1. In the beginning, I'm excited and I'm already visualizing my screenshot moment after I've typed THE END. For a social media post, of course.
2. Usually, I'm off to the races on the outline, which comes fast and furious. This is followed by (again, in most cases) "easy words."
3. Then comes the point when the shiny has worn off. At this point, I follow these three steps for the first of many times:
   a. I review my production schedule and put my progress into perspective.
   b. I remind myself why I wanted to write the book in the first place.
   c. I take a quick glance at other projects to remind myself *I can do this one, too.*
4. I keep my daily writing appointments with myself, even if that cursor does nothing but stare back at me.
5. I keep writing *until.*

Number 5 can last for a while. I rarely finish my first drafts by my target date. Some are early; most are a day late. One is still "in progress" after waaaay too long! But—and here's a big but that might help you—I refuse to give up. There's no way I just decide to not complete a project, no matter how many times I have to come back to it, figure out what the heck I was thinking the last time I touched it, and press the reset button.

Why?

Because here's the truth: You won't reach your prosperous potential if you don't complete the project and get it out into the world. Plan to work on your first draft until it's finished, because when you do, you'll be able to turn it into a revenue-generating asset! ∎

Honorée Corder

How to Make Millions with Marketing

It is better to focus on selling the books you have written than it is to write the next book.

How's that for a controversial statement? Obviously, if you have only one or two books under your belt, it probably won't hold true. However, for those working on their second trilogy or with a backlist in the high single digits or more, it's a reality—even more so if you've written dozens of books. And I'm going to convince you why.

What is your monthly sales figure? Wouldn't you like to double it before you write the next book? Time and time again, I have taken a pause in my writing schedule, delved into the analysis side of my marketing strategies, and increased my income by a sizable percentage.

You can too. I have proven this with other authors.

Let's say you have written X number of books. You are dabbling with some ads on Facebook and Amazon, maybe running a paid promotion here and there, and you are selling $Y worth of books a month. You just need more books, right?

Adding another book gives you an average Z percent more product on the market. The more books you have, the smaller Z becomes. But if instead of plunging straight into your next project, you instead focus on figuring out advertising and marketing for your existing books, you can make 100 percent more money. Maybe 200 percent. Heck, it could be 1,000 percent.

That's what I did, and I was not the first nor the last to figure out this equation.

When I gave some real thought to how it ought to be advertised, I generated six times more sales between one month and the next. It was book 1 in a series, and you can imagine what this did to my overall income from the subsequent books.

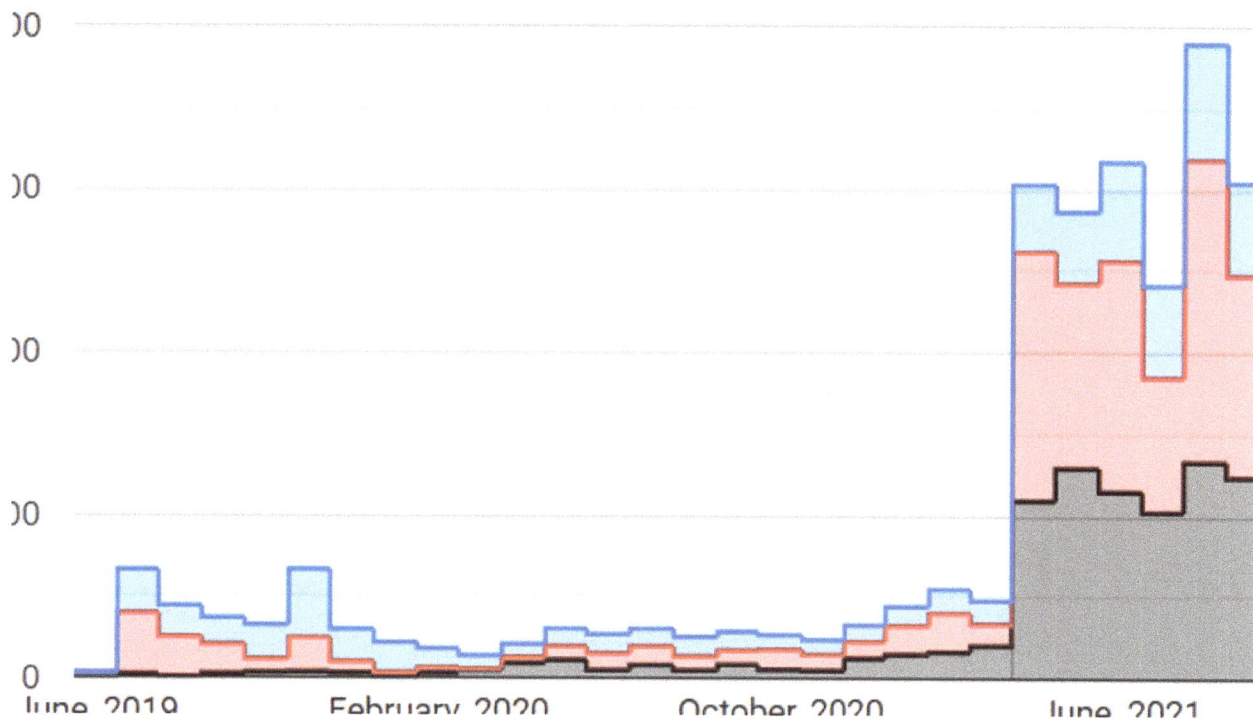

Figure 1.

When I gave some real thought to how the first book in my series ought to be advertised, I generated six times more sales between one month and the next.

How? I learned to use Facebook advertising. Yup, that's pretty much it. There are multiple platforms out there for marketing your work—Facebook, Amazon, BookBub—and over the coming months, I plan to show you how to be successful with all of them. However, I urge you to focus on one for now.

Learn one, get it right, and when it is doing what you need it to do, then consider another option.

Maybe you are selling lots of books without advertising. It happens for some people. They write something great, they nail the cover, and the book flies. But for how long? If this describes you, how will you maintain sales when they start to dip? What are you doing about sales of your backlist?

For most authors, the very simple equation is that you need to spend money to make money. You can do lots for free: newsletter swaps, grouped promotions on sites like BookFunnel or StoryOrigin. Some will have success with such tactics. But I do not know anyone who achieves sustained sales over the years without paying to advertise. ■

Steve Higgs

Stretch It Out

SIMPLE YOGA POSES TO TRY FROM YOUR CHAIR

As an independent writer, poring over your work, you surely maintain peak physical performance. After all, our bodies are the vessel by which we create art, right? Most likely, this isn't the case, and between writing sprints and hours of editing, you've likely experienced aches in places you never knew you could. This is the burden we bear as writers chained to a desk.

Luckily, there are solutions that don't require vacating your sacred grounds and don't require a huge allotment of time. Chair yoga was seemingly conceived for the busy writer, and these asanas—yoga-speak for poses—can help with mobility and strength. It should always be noted, however, that before exercising, consult your doctor or other medical professional. The benefits of exercise are unique to the exerciser, and therefore, finding the right exercises to fit your lifestyle takes precedence.

With some basic know-how and a will to address the creaky joints and random pains, simple exercises can have a long-term impact. When your sprint timer dials down, consider these five simple stretches you can do at your desk to protect your posture and keep your writing machine chugging along.

Images by: Verywell/Ben Goldstein

Seated Forward Bend

Seated Eagle

Wrist Stretch

FIVE SIMPLE STRETCHES

Hold these poses for five seconds and increase the time as you desire. The first few stretches target tension in your back whereas the last few help your hands and wrists. Do them throughout the day to promote good posture. Don't feel pressured to perform these exercises with rigid form. They should be modified for those with mobility issues, so do them as you're able and to your preferred comfort level.

Cat-Cow Stretch: On an inhale, arch your back and look up. On an exhale, round your spine and let your head drop forward.

Seated Forward Bend: Interlace your fingers behind your back and straighten your arms, then draw your fingers down. Fold at the waist and bring your hands over your back.

Seated Spinal Twist: Turn so you are sitting sideways in your chair. Twist toward the back.

Seated Eagle: Wrap your right leg over your left. Bring your arms forward and cross until your palms touch. Lift your elbows.

Wrist Stretch: Stand up and place your palms on the edge of your desk. Turn your hands so your wrists face your keyboard. Lean away with your arms straight, flattening your palms as much as possible. ■

David Viergutz

Keep the Gold

WHAT TO CONSIDER WHEN 'SHINY OBJECT SYNDROME' THREATENS YOUR WORK-IN-PROGRESS

Having a surge of creativity can be a great feeling. Everywhere you look, you seem to find new ideas. But while this can be exciting, it can also make it draining to progress in your current work. Your half-written drafts will be dropped. You may feel tempted to delete your unfinished book and run off with another idea because it sounds better.

Writing is a game of commitment. You have to focus on a project and finish it before starting another.

At the same time, new ideas make a creative writer; you don't want to throw them away. You never know when that new idea could be more worthwhile to pursue than your current work.

As with anything, it's all about balance.

If you continually find yourself tempted to drift away from your current work and toward some other project, first, understand that you are not alone. Plenty of writers have struggled with this dilemma. You also need to be honest about what's important to you in the long run. Is the new idea worth it? Will it be rewarding?

Try keeping a record of your new ideas with the promise that you'll come back to them when done with your current story. If the temptation to find something new persists, ask yourself why you might feel more motivated by a new project and whether there's something preventing you from making progress with your current manuscript.

Maybe it's time for a break from the current story and to stretch your brain with something new. That doesn't make you a bad writer. Sometimes you'll feel better and more knowledgeable when you come back to old writing after taking up new ideas.

Different things work for different people, and it's up to you to decide what's best for yourself. Weigh your choices, decide what aligns with your goals in the long run, and recognize that "shiny object" glinting from beside your current work-in-progress could just be a distraction. But it could also be gold that's ready to be unearthed. ◼

Comfort Amaechi

In This Issue

Executive Team

Chelle Honiker, Publisher

As the publisher of Indie Author Magazine, Chelle Honiker brings nearly three decades of startup, technology, training, and executive leadership experience to the role. She's a serial entrepreneur, founding and selling multiple successful companies including a training development company, travel agency, website design and hosting firm, a digital marketing consultancy, and a wedding planning firm. She's organized and curated multiple TEDx events and hired to assist other nonprofit organizations as a fractional executive, including The Travel Institute and The Freelance Association.

As a writer, speaker, and trainer she believes in the power of words and their ability to heal, inspire, incite, and motivate. Her greatest inspiration is her daughters, Kelsea and Cathryn, who tolerate her tendency to run away from home to play with her friends around the world for months at a time. It's said she could run a small country with just the contents of her backpack.

Alice Briggs, Creative Director

As the creative director of Indie Author Magazine, Alice Briggs utilizes her more than three decades of artistic exploration and expression, business startup adventures, and leadership skills. A serial entrepreneur, she has started several successful businesses. She brings her experience in creative direction, magazine layout and design, and graphic design in and outside of the indie author community to her role.

With a masters of science in Occupational Therapy, she has a broad skill set and uses it to assist others in achieving their desired goals. As a writer, teacher, healer, and artist, she loves to see people accomplish all they desire. She's excited to see how IAM will encourage many authors to succeed in whatever way they choose. She hopes to meet many of you in various places around the world once her passport is back in use.

Nicole Schroeder, Editor in Chief

Nicole Schroeder is a storyteller at heart. As the editor in chief of Indie Author Magazine, she brings nearly a decade of journalism and editorial experience to the publication, delighting in any opportunity to tell true stories and help others do the same. She holds a bachelor's degree from the Missouri School of Journalism and minors in English and Spanish. Her previous work includes editorial roles at local publications, and she's helped edit and produce numerous fiction and nonfiction books, including a Holocaust survivor's memoir, alongside independent publishers. Her own creative writing has been published in national literary magazines. When she's not at her writing desk, Nicole is usually in the saddle, cuddling her guinea pigs, or spending time with family. She loves any excuse to talk about Marvel movies and considers National Novel Writing Month its own holiday.

Monthly Columnists

Honorée Corder

Honorée Corder is the author of more than fifty books, an empire builder, and encourager of writers. When she's not writing, she's spoiling her dog and two cats, eating something fabulous her husband made on the grill, working out, or reading. She hopes this article made a positive impact on your life, and if it did, you'll reach out to her via HonoreeCorder.com.

Craig Martelle

High school Valedictorian enlists in the Marine Corps under a guaranteed tank contract. An inauspicious start that was quickly superseded by excelling in language study. Contract waived, a year at the Defense Language Institute to learn Russian and off to keep my ears on the big red machine during the Soviet years. Earned a four-year degree in two years by majoring in Russian Language. My general staff. career included choice side gigs – UAE, Bahrain, Korea, Russia, and Ukraine.

Major Martelle. I retired from the Marines after a couple years at the embassy in Moscow working arms control issues.

Department of Homeland Security then law school next. I was working for a high-end consulting firm performing business diagnostics, business law, and leadership coaching. For the money they paid me, I was good with that. Just until I wasn't. Then I started writing.

Steve Higgs

"When Steve Higgs wrote his debut novel, he was a Captain in the British Army. He would love to pretend that he had one of those careers that has to be redacted and in general denied by the government. In truth though, he started out as a mechanic. Not like Jason Statham, sneaking about as a contract killer, more like one of those greasy gits who charge you a fortune and keep your car for a week when all you went in for was a squeaky door hinge.

Now retired from the military, he is having a ball writing mystery stories and crime thrillers and claims to have more than a hundred books forming an unruly queue in his head as they clamour to get out. He lives in the south-east corner of England with a duo of lazy sausage dogs. Surrounded by rolling hills, brooding castles, and vineyards, he doubts he will ever leave."

Writers

Comfort Amaechi

Comfort Amaechi is a rising Content Writer with more than 3 years of experience.

She has written for different niches which makes her a versatile writer.

Also, She is a tech enthusiast and is tech-savvy with knowledge of using different software to increase productivity and help businesses.

She has taught more than 100 people the skill of writing and she aims to help businesses position and grow with her writing skill.

Victoria Blisse

Victoria Blisse is known as the Queen of Smut, Reverend to the kinky and is Head of Fetish.com's BDSM training school. She is a well-known content writer of all things kink and has 15 years' experience in the world of erotic publishing. Victoria runs Smut Market with her husband, Kev and is a well-known face in the Manchester BDSM scene.

Mancunian Odd Duck, her northern English quirkiness shows through in all of her stories and poems along with her own particular brand of humour and romance that bring laughs and warm fuzzies in equal measure.

Passion, love and laughter fill her works, just as they fill her busy life.

Find out all about Victoria's sexy shenanigans and sensual stories at Victoriablisse.co.uk and follow her on Facebook, Instagram and Twitter.

Heather Clement Davis

Heather Clement Davis has twenty-six years' experience in museums, archaeology, art, counseling, art therapy, creative writing, and nonprofit management. She holds enough graduate work to make a Ph.D. cry as her neurodivergent brain is hooked on learning everything. She's currently a masters candidate in Arts Management. Her paintings and pottery are in galleries and collections worldwide and her poetry and her nonfiction and fiction has found its way to literary journals around the U.S. When not writing or making art, Heather can be found playing Catan or watching Star Trek with her family.

Sharon Dooley

Sharon Kay Dooley is a semi-retired Registered Nurse who has been a writer since her high school days. Sharon loves word games, Wordle, and puzzles. She has always been a reader and reads everything except horror and most Sci-fi. Currently, she is writing a series of children's books and an environmentally based cozy mystery series.

Since she lives in MD near the nation's capital, she keeps an eye on politics and the Washington Football Team-The Commanders. She includes among her special favorites her two children, and her grandchildren. Other likes are cooking, drinking excellent coffee, eating chocolate desserts, and walks with her rescue dog.

Gill Fernley

Gill Fernley writes fiction in several genres under different pen names, but what all of them have in common is humor and romance, because she can't resist a happy ending or a good laugh. She's also a freelance content writer and has been running her own business since 2013. Before that, she was a technical author and documentation manager for an engineering company and can describe to you more than you'd ever wish to know about airflow and filtration in downflow booths. Still awake? Wow, that's a first! Anyway, that experience taught her how to explain complex things in straightforward language and she hopes it will come in handy for writing articles for IAM. Outside of writing, she's a cake decorator, expert shoe hoarder, and is fluent in English, dry humor and procrastibaking.

Audrey Hughey

Audrey Hughey designs planners, writes fiction, and works diligently to help her fellow authors. Although she currently writes horror and thrillers, she's as eclectic in her writing tastes as in her reading. When she's not submerged in the worlds of fiction and nonfiction, she's caring for her family, enjoying nature, or finding more ways to bring a little more light into the world.

Jenn Lessmann

Jenn Lessmann is the author of three stories published on Amazon's Kindle Vella, two unpublished novels, and a blog that tests Pinterest hacks in the real world (where supplies are sometimes limited, and all projects are overseen by children with digital attention spans). A former barista, stage manager, and high school English teacher with advanced degrees from impressive colleges, she continues to drink excessive amounts of caffeine, stay up later than is absolutely necessary, and read three or four books at a time. She loves lists and the rule of three. Irony too. Jenn is currently studying witchcraft and the craft of writing, and giggling internally whenever they intersect. She writes snarky (not spicy) paranormal fantasy for new adults whenever her dog will allow it.

Megan Linski-Fox

Megan Linski lives in Michigan. She is a USA TODAY Bestselling Author and the author of more than fifty novels. She has over fifteen years of experi-ence writing books alongside working as a journalist and editor. She graduated from the University of Iowa, where she studied Creative Writing.

Grace Snoke

Grace Snoke is a 42-year-old author and personal assistant residing in Lincoln, Nebraska. Having been a corporate journalist for more than a decade and a video game journalist for even longer, writing has been something she has always enjoyed doing. In addition to non-fiction books, she is currently working on a paranormal romance series, and two urban fantasy series under her real name. She has also released more than a dozen illustrated children's books and several non-fiction books. She has been publishing erotica under a pen name since 2017. For more information about her personal assistant business visit: https://spider-webzdesign.net. Her author site is: https://gracesnoke.com.

David Viergutz

David Viergutz is a disabled Army Veteran, Law Enforcement Veteran, husband and proud father. He is an author of stories from every flavor of horror and dark fiction. One day, David's wife sat him down and gave him the confidence to start putting his imagination on paper. From then on out his creativity has no longer been stifled by self-doubt and he continues to write with a smile on his face in a dark, candle-lit room.

Ready to level up your indie author career?

Trick question. Of course you are.

*INDIE
^Author Tools

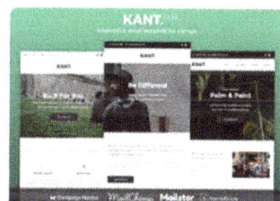

PUBLISHERROCKET

FIND
PROFITABLE
KINDLE
KEYWORDS

Book Marketing Research
Made Simple!

writelink.to/pubrocket

www.ingramcontent.com/pod-product-compliance
Lightning Source LLC
Chambersburg PA
CBHW052344210326
41597CB00037B/6252